RED HOT Presentations

HOW TO WRITE AND DELIVER A TALK SO YOU GET MORE CLIENTS, MAKE MORE MONEY, AND BECOME FAMOUS IN YOUR NICHE AS A SPEAKER

JUDY COHEN

Printed in the United States of America

First Printing, 2013

ISBN 978-0-9898277-0-6

Red Hot Presentations Press
Publisher@RedHotPresentations.com

www.RedHotPresentations.com

Cover Design by Studio West

Quantity Sales Ordering Information:
Special discounts are available on quantity purchases by corporations, associations, and others. For details, contact the publisher at the email address above.

Dedicated to my husband Jeff, and
my children Stefan and Beth,
the brightest stars in my universe.

CONTENTS

Acknowledgments   *ix*

Foreword   *xi*

Introduction   **1**
Who This Book Is For   2
My Story   3
Speak Now   8

ACT 1: PREPARE

1   **Become A Little Bit Famous**   **11**
Hometown Celebrity   13
"Are You Famous In Your Niche?" Quiz   19
Key Points To Remember   22
Action Items   23

2   **Audition For Speaking Parts**   **25**
Casting Call   27
You Got The Part!   28
Get The Hook!   33
Your Signature Speech   34
Deleted Scenes   36
Key Points To Remember   37
Action Items   39

3 Stage Fright   **41**

The Show Must Go On   42

Practice, Practice, Practice   45

Controlling Fear   48

Your Authentic Voice   51

Stage Presence   51

Key Points To Remember   56

Action Items   58

4 Red Carpet Ready   **59**

Your Image   60

Wardrobe   61

Accessories   63

Attitude   65

Hair   66

Makeup   66

Photos   67

Video   67

One Sheet   68

Key Points To Remember   69

Action Items   70

ACT 2: PRESENT

5 Showtime   **73**

Arrive Early   74

Lights, Camera, Action   76

Know Your Opening Lines 78

Key Points To Remember 81

Action Items 82

6 Red Hot Presentations 83

Coming Attractions 84

Connect With Your Audience 85

Delivery 87

Show & Tell 89

Non-Verbal Messages 90

Key Points To Remember 92

Action Items 93

7 Set The Scene 95

Storytelling 95

Key Points To Remember 99

Action Items 100

8 Movie Credits 101

Don't Bore Your Audience 103

Visuals 103

Key Points To Remember 108

Action Items 109

9 Questions and Answers 111

Handling Q&A 112

Key Points To Remember 116

Action Items 118

ACT 3: PROFIT

10	**Selling From The Stage**	**121**
	Fan Club	122
	Making An Offer	123
	Key Points To Remember	127
	Action Items	128
11	**It's A Wrap**	**129**
	Strong Close	130
	A Star Is Born	131
	Encore	132
	Key Points To Remember	134
	Action Items	135
	About The Author	**137**
	Speaking	137
	Red Hot Presentations Programs	138
	A Gift For You	139

ACKNOWLEDGMENTS

Writing a book is not a solitary journey. Like an actor who stars on stage, there is always help behind the curtain. It is with gratitude and appreciation that I thank the people who worked their magic offstage.

Geoffrey Berwind, professional storyteller, consultant and trainer, thank you for writing the foreword to this book. Your expertise in helping authors, speakers, experts and companies identify, craft and tell their stories made you the perfect person to set the stage for this book. Your insight shows the magic that can happen when speakers use stories to share their message. Thank you for helping me learn how to use stories effectively.

To my husband Jeff Thompson, thank you for your time in laboriously reading and editing the many pages of written copy. Your revisions and suggestions made the book better. I could not have done as well without you.

To Louise Adams, my designer and friend, thank you for the beautiful book cover. You brought my vision to life. It was a pleasure working with someone who knew exactly what I wanted to create in the form of design.

To my children, Stefan and Beth Cohen, thank you for your love and support. Your belief in me makes everything possible.

FOREWORD

It's every speaker's nightmare.

You're in the light, on the stage, facing a room full of people sitting there in the dark. Perhaps they've been told to be there by their boss or perhaps you are offering a workshop or speech to a big company. They're sitting there, expecting to be enlightened (hoping to be entertained and not bored to death) by what you are about to say.

Maybe this is not your usual speaking opportunity, but *this* presentation is one that might really propel your career to the next level. Perhaps there are people in the audience who you really want to impress - and this is no time for anything less than, well, a "red hot presentation." The question is, are you ready? Have you properly prepared? Have you crafted the speech in just the right way to connect with your audience?

That's the key word, isn't it? CONNECT. That's what great speakers do.

I've worked for years as a professional storytelling consultant and coach. I've trained hundreds of presenters in how to craft and tell their real-life stories in order to ace their speeches, and if I had to distill the core mission to a great presentation, it is this: your speech really isn't *your* speech at all. Yes, you're delivering it and, yes, it's the result of your accumulated work experiences, research and expertise.

But...a great speech is actually a shared experience between you and your audience. A great speech or as Judy calls it, a red hot presentation, is designed and delivered so that you and your audience are truly connecting. And, connecting on many levels: through the head, through the gut and most especially, through the heart. I've learned that we process information through those three key areas: the head is the receiving system for data, facts, numbers, statistics – this is where we think and process information. Our gut is the place where we listen to our instincts and our intuitions. Our heart is our emotional processing place: where we feel, where we are authentic and where we connect.

This is why the ability to properly tell stories is a core component of a great speech. We humans have engaged with stories as far back as we go, while modern data are just that – modern, recent and not really how we're wired to relate to the world. Speakers who take the time to really *think* ahead of time about who their audience is – what their needs are (and, by needs I mean both professionally and as human beings) and tailor their presentation to that – these are the speakers who become celebrities in their niche.

Your niche may simply be in becoming better known in your own company by offering a powerful presentation for your colleagues or staff. If you're an author or entrepreneur, you are trying to connect with your target market and so want to have them feel that they relate to you. Judy's idea of becoming a "hometown celebrity" is designed to address this powerful marketing concept.

You know what I love about dogs? You're always a celebrity to them. Unlike other types of pets (who shall remain nameless lest I be accused to bias), dogs are totally into you, 24/7, 365 days a year. YOU are their niche.

So imagine your customers, clients, colleagues, audiences to feeling about you the way your dog does: you're a rock star and always will be.

That's why Judy has created this book, which distills her experience and her strategies. She is on a mission to end ho-hum speaking and she wants to take you to the next level when you present. Her unique combination of wisdom, experience, warmth and creativity is just what is needed. I invite you to open yourself to what Judy has to teach you so that you become a great speaker... every time. Enjoy!

Geoffrey Berwind
Professional Storytelling Consultant & Trainer

INTRODUCTION

This is it. The day you prepared for has arrived. You know what you are going to say, you look the part and you are ready to make your entrance. You confidently step out on stage. The audience rivets their attention on you.

You deliberately pause and hold the audience captive in the silence before you begin to speak. They are spellbound as you communicate your message. You bring them to the edge of their seats and leave them wanting more.

At the end of your presentation you hear "bravo" and thunderous applause as the audience jumps to their feet. This is your shining moment. You are a Speaker. You are a Star.

Who This Book Is For

This book is for you if you want to be recognized as an expert in your area of specialty. If you are ready to go from unknown to center stage and be known as an expert in your field, you are about to learn how speaking can help you become the new face of celebrity. It will change the way you think about yourself and your business. In a short amount of time you can go from unknown to a little bit famous as a speaker in your niche.

I am going to give you a backstage pass so you can have a behind the scenes look at what goes into crafting and delivering a speech that will make you memorable. You will learn how to position yourself as a star in your niche through the art of presenting. You will gain insight into how to write and deliver a talk so you stay top-of-mind, have raving fans, and become sought after in your area of expertise.

If you are ready to use speaking to grow your business, this book will give you the tools and knowledge you seek.

My Story

At this point in my life, I can tell you that speaking is a powerful way to share your message and get noticed. But I can also tell you that speaking was not always something I found easy to do.

Here's a question I'd like you to answer. "Have you ever felt so fearful about speaking up that you just shut down?" Well, at one time, that was me. Today I'm considered an expert in the field of presenting, but I wasn't always this way.

I experienced a tough childhood and as a result shut down, becoming afraid of people and public situations. I lost my ability to voice opinions. Being resilient, I survived those early years and eventually put myself through college and got a degree in marketing. After graduation I was hired as a Marketing Associate.

It turned out that I did really good work and began to excel. I was excited by the campaigns I created. Several months after starting my new job I entered an awards competition held by the Philadelphia Direct Marketing Association.

I attended the awards ceremony, eager to see the marketing campaigns produced by my esteemed colleagues. I watched as many awards were distributed. And then I heard it, "The Benjamin Franklin Benny Award for Direct Marketing Excellence goes to Judy Cohen." I won the highest honor of recognition bestowed by the association. Many marketers work a full career and never earn that prestigious award.

Arriving at work the next morning, the Vice President of Marketing presented me with flowers on behalf of the company. He was thrilled that I brought acclaim to the organization. Several days later he called me into his office. As I sat facing him he said, "Your work is exemplary, but you won't rise in this company if you don't learn to speak up."

My ancient fears filled me as I heard him say that I should verbally share my ideas. I was silent. The only sound I could hear was the beating of my heart. We sat there looking at each other for a while. Finally he broke the silence. "I will groom you." I couldn't believe my ears. Someone in authority believed in me!

The Vice President became my coach and my mentor. In meetings when a point was discussed or a question would be asked, he would stand behind me and whisper in my ear, "Speak now." Speak now. I remember so vividly this kind man saying those two little words. Just two little words, which gave me the permission to speak that I never got before.

The VP continued to coach me and encourage me with "Speak now." It was hard at first, but I tried. I spoke up and people listened. They responded positively to my statements and nothing bad happened to me. I learned to walk through my fear and finally, after all those years, I had found my voice.

As I spoke into my newly born confidence, my career soared. Soon, I was rapidly promoted to Marketing Manager and my salary doubled. I shared campaign strategies with C level executives, met with the sales department, and focused on company initiatives. I was promoted to Marketing Director with a 6 figure salary. I meet weekly with the CEO, I addressed the employees in monthly company meetings, and I conducted an orientation program for new hires. And, most importantly, I was finally *happy*. I had found my voice. I was no longer shut down.

To my surprise, I found another outlet for my voice – acting.

I auditioned for a repertory theater group and became a member of the ensemble cast. We put on plays for children. I can still hear the sound of the children's laughter and their high pitched squeals of delight. They were enthralled by the characters that stood on stage and they got lost in the stories that sparked their imagination.

I joined the professional actor's union and performed as a background extra in many of the movies that were filmed in my geographic area. I was in scenes with Danny DeVito, Joe Piscopo, Penn and Teller, and many others. It was an education watching these stars deliver their lines and bring their characters to life. It was also exciting being in scenes directed by film industry greats like Brian De Palma.

Having found my voice, and remembering my early days when I was encouraged to "Speak now," I interviewed with an executive producer to appear on a television talk show. She told me, "If you are good, I'll give you one show, if you are great, I'll give you a series." I put together concepts that would leave their audience wanting more. I landed the series. It was a huge success with the viewers. The program brought me opportunities to appear on other television shows and radio.

My big claim to fame occurred when I filmed a television commercial for a local radio station. I can still hear the director saying to me, "Judy Cohen, you are my star!" The commercial aired three times an hour, every day, for a year. I was recognized everywhere. I became a hometown celebrity. A major metropolitan newspaper interviewed me and several others who appeared in the commercial. The journalist discussed the raving fans we had because of the television exposure.

Becoming a hometown celebrity made all the difference in the choices I would make. It profoundly impacted my career. Empowered by my success, I started my company, Red Hot Presentations. I help those who feel shut down realize that if they learn to speak up, they too can have an incredible career, position themselves as an expert, and find their authentic voice.

My love for acting translated into creating my coaching program for aspiring speakers. I love helping entrepreneurs become famous in their areas of expertise. I do this by teaching my clients how to write and deliver empowering speeches.

So again I ask, "Have you ever felt so fearful about speaking up that you just shut down?" Well, I've committed my life to helping people who feel that way learn to speak up and become famous in their niche by learning how to become the speaker everyone remembers.

What I want to do is stand behind YOU and say: "Speak now."

Speak Now

Now it is my turn to guide you. This book on speaking will take you into the land of possibility. I offer you a front row seat to my 3 act play: Prepare, Present and Profit.

The curtain is going up.

ACT 1: PREPARE

CHAPTER 1
BECOME A LITTLE BIT FAMOUS

The day was magnificent. It was one of those days that you hope will last forever. The sky was a soft blue, joined only by a few white clouds. The weather was comfortable. It wasn't warm or cold. It was the perfect temperature where you enjoy being outdoors. I drove into Philadelphia, parked my car and walked rapidly to my appointment on the Parkway. I had recently auditioned for a commercial for a radio station and today was the day we were doing the shoot.

As I arrived I saw people, lights and cameras everywhere. Trailers dotted the landscape. I was just in time to see actress Teri Garr, of *Young*

Frankenstein fame, finish her scene and enter her trailer. I signed in and went to the waiting area. The opportunity to be in a commercial with Teri Garr filled me with exhilaration.

Soon it was my turn to tape my segment of the commercial. The producer started by asking me questions about why I liked the radio station the commercial was promoting. As I talked and shared my thoughts, the cameras rolled. The producer was clearly excited by what I said. "Judy Cohen you are my star! I am going to get the Creative Director and see if we can do an additional segment with you." After watching me on camera, the Creative Director gave the green light for me to keep taping.

Several months later my phone rang. An excited friend was on the line shouting, "I just saw you on TV!" With excitement and anticipation I hoped that I would see the commercial air. And air it did. The spot ran every day for a year, 3 times an hour, every hour, on major stations and cable.

People recognized me at the mall, in restaurants, in libraries. Wherever I went in my hometown I was a familiar face. Speaking made me a hometown celebrity. People approached me and asked about the commercial. A Philadelphia newspaper wrote about the crazy frenzy that the commercial created. Several people in the commercial were interviewed and I was one of them. The newspaper headline proclaimed we had fans.

Hometown Celebrity

Have you ever dreamed of being a little bit famous by being known as an expert in your field? Perhaps you've never given it any thought. Or maybe you recently started a business and are looking for a way to stand out and separate yourself from your competition. Whatever your situation, being an accomplished speaker can help you shine attention on what you do and who you are.

Being a hometown celebrity in your niche is like starring in an Off-Broadway show. You don't have to be globally famous to have your name in lights. You can make your mark on the small part of the world that wants to hear your message. The best part is that you have the hometown advantage. You are one of them. You'll earn the support of others in your town because they will believe you understand their needs.

If you want to take your show on the road and expand your reach, you can, but starting locally will be your easiest access to reaching your target market.

So how can you become a little bit famous? The first step is to make the decision to be known. All of your activities and positioning will stem from this goal. Have a vision of what you would like to create. What will your journey to becoming famous in your niche look like? Imagine. The art of visualization will stir your emotions and fuel your desire.

Fame can change your life. What is the lifestyle you dream about? It is important to know who you are and what you want before you go in search of fame. You need to know your skills and areas needed for improvement.

Honestly assess yourself by answering the following questions.

Who are you?

What makes you special? What makes you different and sets you apart from your competition? What topic, or topics, can you speak on in your area of specialty?

What's your why?

Why do you want fame? What will drive you to

keep going to reach your goal? What benefits will you receive? When you have a strong why, nothing will stop you from taking action and moving forward every day.

How often do you want to speak?

Speak everywhere that fits your schedule, is within your defined geographic area, and is appropriate for your message and your audience. Eventually you may share the stage with big name presenters. You will be in the promotion pieces along with them. When that happens, you will be a little bit famous just through connection! One day you may be the headliner – the keynote speaker. It will be your name in lights on the marquee – or at least in the program. In Chapter 2 we will discuss looking for, and landing, speaking gigs.

How comfortable are you when speaking in front of an audience?

If you have doubts as to whether you can overcome stage fright and speak to audiences large or small, fear not. I will go in depth on this topic in Chapter 3 and give you the information you need to step into your confidence. You are going to discover that your speech is not about you.

How will you stand out?

Decide on your image. Celebrities don't fade into the background. How can your look differentiate you from your competition? Create a memorable public image that is in alignment with your message and personality. You will want to promote your image in all that you do. This includes your marketing materials, website, and when you make personal appearances. We will discuss this topic in detail in Chapter 4.

How do you want to connect with your audience when you step on stage?

Knowing the secret to creating instant audience engagement is what separates beginning speakers from more seasoned presenters. Chapter 5 will show you techniques on how to craft and deliver an opening statement that will determine if your audience tunes in or tunes out.

How do you want to communicate with your audience beyond the spoken word?

You will engage with your audience in a variety of ways. How does your message lend itself to props, visual aids, and body language? Many times the non-spoken form of communication is stronger than the spoken word. We will explore these methods of communication in Chapter 6.

What's your story?

People have an emotional connection to stories. Your personal story is the most important story you can share. It's how you'll be remembered. Talk about yourself in a way that will have people wanting to hear more. Create some buzz about yourself. You never want to be generic. We will look closely at story development in Chapter 7.

How will you keep your audience engaged when you use PowerPoint Slides?

It's not enough to know your content. You need to know how to make your content interesting for your audience the entire time you are speaking.

You are about to learn the techniques that will keep your audience's attention when you use PowerPoint slides. A bored audience will tune out or leave.

In Chapter 8 you will learn how to keep attendees awake and engaged.

How will you handle questions and answers?

Many new speakers are frightened by questions. With preparation the Q&A session can be handled with ease. In Chapter 9 we will discuss how to prepare to answer questions, when to open the room to questions, what to do if you are unable to answer a question, and much more. The goal is to continue positioning yourself as the expert.

What is the cause you support?

Position yourself for the role you want. If you could be known for one thing, what would it be? Think big. Play big. As my husband always says, "Big dreams don't cost anymore." This is your dream. Step into the role and claim it.

In order to connect with you, people need to buy into why you do what you do. It needs to feel right for them. Talk about what you believe and you'll attract those that believe in your message. That's how you'll grow a fan base. It's not about going after everyone. We'll look at growing a fan club in Chapter 10.

We'll also look at ways to create a talk that generates a fan base and promotes selling from the stage. Can you picture selling your book at the back of the room after a speaking engagement and autographing your book for the person who bought it? A well-crafted persuasive presentation can put you on the road to fame and fortune.

Are You A Star In The Making?

Being a little bit famous has enormous benefits. You will get more opportunities when you are known. You will eventually get higher speaking fees and subsequently be in a position of influence.

Celebrities attract opportunities without having to constantly look for work. They get attention and have visibility. Their phones ring off the hook. They aren't in continuous pursuit of new clients. People want to work with them, be near them, get photographed with them, and get their autograph.

In Chapter 11 we will look at my definition of a STAR and how you can continue to shine a light on your area of expertise. Keep reading because you are going to bring that goal into the realm of possibility.

"Are You Famous in Your Niche?" Quiz

Let's start by assessing your current star status with my "Are You Famous in Your Niche?" quiz.

Answer yes or no to the questions below:

Do you have a strong public image, keeping you top-of-mind when a prospect needs someone with your expertise?

Yes_____ No_____

Do you have raving fans offering a constant flow of referrals?

Yes_____ No_____

Do clients call you, eliminating the need for cold calls?

Yes_____ No_____

Do you have a full calendar for your services?

Yes_____ No_____

Do you have a waiting list for your programs or services?

Yes_____ No_____

Scoring: Count your number of "Yes" responses.

0-1: It's time to change your approach and reach for the stars.

2-3: You are on your way to being a little bit famous.

4-5: You are a Superstar!

Don't worry if you had less "yes" answers than you would like. You are only starting on this journey. Just keep in mind that if you are willing to do the work, you can stand out from the crowd and make a name for yourself.

You are now ready to learn how to share your gifts with the world – or at least your niche in your hometown.

It's time to become a little bit famous!

KEY POINTS TO REMEMBER

• You can become a little bit famous. Being a speaker can shine attention on what you do and who you are.

• You can make your mark on the small part of the world that wants to hear your message.

• Make the decision to be known.

• Create a buzz about yourself.

• Have a vision of what you would like to create through speaking.

• Honestly assess what sets you apart from your competition.

• Determine what will drive you to reach your goal.

• Decide on the cause you want to support.

• Create an image that will differentiate you from your competition.

• Speak everywhere that fits your schedule, is within your defined geographic area, and is appropriate for your message and your audience.

ACTION ITEMS

• Make a list of everyone you know and tell them you are looking for speaking opportunities.

• Take my "Are You Famous in Your Niche?" quiz.

CHAPTER 2
AUDITION FOR SPEAKING PARTS

I often look back at my early auditions and smile. I remember the first call I received from the agency representing me. I had an audition for a mattress commercial. My first audition! I dressed for the part based on the instructions I was given and drove to the audition.

I parked my car and walked to the location. I was so excited I felt like I was walking on air. I arrived at an impressive office building, entered the elevator, and watched the numbered floors go by. With great anticipation, I exited the elevator, found the audition room and opened the door.

I can still recall what happened next. I walked through the door and stopped and stared at the sight that greeted me. The room was full of women that looked just like me! There we were. Twenty something, brunette with shoulder length hair, about the same height and weight, in similar dress.

What? Wasn't I unique? I realized the production company knew exactly the type of look they wanted. Unfortunately, I didn't know how to differentiate myself and I didn't get the part.

My next audition had a similar scenario, but this time I was prepared. I was auditioning for a major pharmaceutical print ad. They wanted someone to play the part of a child care worker. During the audition I mentioned the jobs I held working with children. Suddenly I became more interesting. I stood apart from the sea of women that looked like me. I positioned myself as knowledgeable and skilled in working with children. I got the part.

Fast forward twenty years. I took a position as a Marketing Director. When I walked into the office the first day, the Office Manager stared at me. The stare was so intense she made me uncomfortable. Finally she said, "Your picture is hanging in my home." This time it was my turn to stare. I walked closer to her and asked, "What did you say?" She asked if I ever did a pharmaceutical print ad. When

I told her I had, she replied, "That was my son that was sitting on your lap in the ad." We were both amazed that we were together again after all those years. I was amazed that she recognized me. She told me how she loved the way I had interacted with her son. My takeaway: Be unique. Be memorable.

So how will you stand apart from your competition? Are you one of many people offering the same service? How will you be unique and memorable in your way? This is an important question to answer. Find a way to position yourself and stand apart from your competition.

Casting Call

The first step to becoming known as a speaker in your area of expertise is to audition for the part. You need to answer the "casting calls" and go after speaking engagements. To be discovered and become famous in your niche, you need to be visible. You need to get out there and speak.

If you have never spoken before, you are probably wondering where to start. The best way to get comfortable speaking is to start by giving free talks. The local Rotary Clubs, Lion's Clubs,

Chambers of Commerce, women's organizations, and places of worship, are always looking for speakers for their meetings. Research groups in your local area and find the ones that would be a good fit for your message.

Who do you know? Make a list of everyone you can think of. You will be amazed at the length of the list! Contact these people, tell them your goal to be a speaker, and that you are looking for speaking opportunities. You will see doors open for you. People you know may be able to connect you with Centers of Influence in your hometown. Ask your contacts what groups they belong to. Many times people will give you leads for speaking opportunities within their organizations.

Once you get leads, contact the organizations. Tell the event planner the topic you speak about and the benefit their group will receive by hearing your talk. Share how you can customize your speech. Your goal is to get them interested in your area of expertise.

You Got The Part!

By consistently following leads, your determination and hard work will pay off. You will land your first speaking engagement.

So what do you do after you get a speech on your calendar? Let's start a deep dive into crafting and delivering an engaging presentation.

Although knowing how to write your speech is critical to your success, writing isn't the first step in the process. The critical first step is knowing your audience.

As a presenter you must determine the purpose of your message *before* crafting your speech. Before taking pen to paper, or typing on the keyboard, it is critical to research the audience that will hear your presentation. You can research the needs of the group by speaking with the organizer. It may even be possible to survey some of the people who will be in attendance. Another avenue is to look for statistics and trends you can discuss that are pertinent to the group.

Your goal is to determine the message that will resonate with your audience and bring it to life. Above all, it must be something they want to hear, not what you think they need to hear. It is only after you know what the audience wants, that you are able to determine the information to share.

Who is the client you want to work with? You want to speak to audiences filled with your ideal client. Do not make the mistake of sharing your message with everyone.

As a speaker, you need to deliver your message to the people in your niche who want to hear what you have to say. If you want to reach builders and you give your speech to florists, your speech on what it takes to make it in the building industry will not resonate with your audience of florists. Yes, there may be content that you deliver that is relevant to both audiences, but it is the specifics addressing their pain points that are the key to have them wanting to hear more. Therefore, the content in your script must be relevant to the specific needs of the audience you are speaking to.

Ask yourself, "Why will they be at the presentation? What message do they want to hear?" Keep your ideal client in mind with every sentence you write. Use language they relate to as it will strengthen your connection. It shows that you understand who they are and the needs they have. As you prepare your speech always answer the audience's question: "Why should I care?" Your speaking points must address their problems with the solutions you offer.

Your message must be clear and easy to grasp. If people are confused, they will stop listening. Stay on topic. Every point you make, activity you select, or story you tell must support your topic. Use short sentences. When you speak in complex sentences you risk losing your listeners. Keep your audience engaged with the use of the word "you." Speak to everyone, but make each audience member feel as if you are talking to them as an individual.

Every person has a different learning style. When you speak to a group, it is important to include activities that address the different ways people learn. If you don't, you risk not reaching all the people in your audience.

Some people are visual learners. They like to be shown how to do something. They respond well to graphic images and props. Auditory learners need things explained to them. They need to hear you describe why a step is important. The audience members that are analytical need to be given examples of how things work. They like to think things through and ponder your examples. You should also create an activity that involves your kinesthetic attendees. Have the audience use physical movement if possible. You can also create audience interaction.

With each point you make, address the different ways people learn. You will not only capture the attention of all the people in your audience, but you will help them increase the retention of your information.

You need to decide if you want to deliver a speech that is an educational presentation or a persuasive presentation. There are differences. An educational presentation is a teaching presentation that offers content only. In this type of speech you want to position yourself as the expert as you teach the material. You want to write a persuasive script if you want to have a call to action toward the end of your speech. In your call to action you will offer your audience the opportunity to work with you or buy your products or services.

In a persuasive presentation you need to seed your offer throughout your speech. Set your sales goal and the outcome you want before writing your script. The points you make throughout your speech should support what you want to sell.

Structure your speech so that you create a desire in people to act on your offer. You want to change their perspective and have them start to believe that you can help them solve their problem. Deliver valuable content during your presentation that offers them some relief in solving that problem. The audience needs to realize that you can't go deep enough to cover all the needed information in 45 minutes. Make the audience understand that your offer will allow you to go deeper into the points you made in your presentation. Create certainty that your product or service will be able to help your audience members solve the problem they have been unable to solve themselves. We will look more at crafting a Call to Action in Chapter 10 of Act 3: PROFIT.

Get The Hook!

It is vital that you have a strong title hook for your speech. A hook is a statement that grabs the attention of your audience, before you begin to speak, and creates a desire to know more. Craft a title that rivals a headline on a tabloid magazine at the checkout line in a supermarket. The title should have a strong promise stating what you will deliver. Your goal is to fulfill the promise of the title during your speech.

Hooks can also be used to create transitions in your speech that leave people wanting to know what you are going to say next. Have you ever watched TV and heard the announcer say something like, "Coming up 5 simple steps to look

10 years younger by tonight" and then they go to commercial? You find yourself sitting through endless commercials because you want to hear what is going to be said. That's the hook. You want to add this drama to your speeches.

Use transitions that hook your audience, bring them to the edge of their seats and leave them wanting to know more.

Your Signature Speech

Most speakers develop a signature speech. It is a speech that represents who they are and the unique message they share. It has their voice, their language, their stories. It's what makes a speaker memorable and allows them to stand apart from their competition.

My signature speech is about helping people become famous in their niche by learning how to become a great speaker. What I want to be known for is creating the new face of celebrity. What's your message? What do you stand for? What are you passionate about? How do you want to be remembered?

Develop a speech you feel comfortable giving that represents what you do and who you are.

Share a message you want people to hear and associate with you. You'll connect strongly with your audience if your message has personal appeal. Find the people who will automatically share your message with others. These people will become your fans. Knowing the type of audience who will resonate with your message will help you identify where to speak.

No matter how many times you give a speech, keep it fresh because it will always be a new experience for your audience. Think of actors in a play. They do the same show over and over, but it is the first time for their audience. Follow this suggestion and you will always have a great performance.

An actor with a poor script can give the best possible performance, but it will still fall flat. The same will happen to a speaker that doesn't have a strong speech. Craft a signature speech that elevates your message and you will be on your way to stardom.

The key is offering valuable content over tons of information. The number of points you will make in your speech will relate to the length of time you are given to speak. Three key points is a good number to aim for in a 45 minute speech. If you have too many points you can't give enough meaningful information on each point. You risk losing your audience as they are not able to retain an overload of information. The fewer the points, the more memorable the speech.

There is a 10 minute rule with regard to attention spans. Every ten minutes change the way you are delivering the information in order to keep your audience from tuning out. Tell a story, do an activity or exercise, or share an interesting fact to drive home your key points. Keep their interest by changing the way you share information on your points throughout your speech.

Deleted Scenes

In movies, there are always deleted scenes. You must do the same with your writing. Edit your speech after you write it and let parts land on the cutting room floor. Your goal is to stay on topic and keep your points to a minimum. Make sure you utilize smooth transitions that hook your audience. Each point should flow into the next. Remove all extraneous content. If you can't part with the content you delete, save it for another speech.

KEY POINTS TO REMEMBER

• Be unique. Be memorable.

• If you want to be discovered and become famous in your niche, you need to be visible.

• Know your audience.

• Determine the purpose of your message *before* crafting your speech.

• Your speech must address something the audience wants to hear, not what you think they need to hear.

• Your message must be clear and easy to understand.

• Use short sentences.

• Every point you make, activity you select, or story you tell must support your topic.

• Make each audience member feel as if you are talking to them individually.

• Always have a strong title hook for your speech.

• Decide on the niche you want to speak to.

• Research the needs of the group you will be speaking to and customize your speech for them.

• Address different learning styles when speaking.

• Decide if your speech will be a persuasive presentation or an educational presentation.

• Use hooks to create transitions in your speech.

• No matter how many times you give a speech, keep it fresh as it is always a new experience for your audience.

• Offer valuable content over tons of information.

• The fewer the points, the more memorable the speech.

• Keep interest by changing the way you share information throughout your speech.

• Edit your speech and remove extraneous content.

ACTION ITEMS

• Look for speaking engagements.

• Develop a signature speech that represents what you do and who you are.

CHAPTER 3
STAGE FRIGHT

I attended a local business networking event that was holding a competition for Marketer of the Year. It was a memorable experience for me because I was fascinated by one of the speakers. Many people entered the contest and presented the marketing results they received over the year. Everyone earned the right to present, but not everyone delivered their message in a way that made me want to vote for them. However, one woman competing for Marketer of the Year stood out from the rest. She was clearly nervous. Her hands were shaking as she handled the visual examples of mailings she wrote and mailed over the year. Her face broke out in blotches. The redness intensified and spread on her face and neck. But she had a strong message to share. Even though she was nervous she staid the course. She was the presenter that I supported with my vote. The woman went on to become Marketer of the Year. She won the contest because she worked through her fear of speaking and shared a message that resonated with her audience.

The Show Must Go On

If you are thinking that you could never do presentations because of your fear of public speaking, I'd like to offer you some thoughts that may be helpful. It's normal to get butterflies when getting up on stage. It happens to most people. It happens to me. It tells me I am in the zone and ready to deliver great content. The nerves vanish as soon as I start speaking and connecting with my audience.

Realize the presentation is always about your audience. It's not about you. I know we worry that people are judging us and we feel vulnerable when we stand before others. What you need to focus on is the fact that giving a speech is about the sharing of information. Your audience doesn't want you to fail. They are investing their time to learn something of benefit to them. It's only about them. They are focusing on what they are getting out of the experience of hearing you speak.

When you feel fearful it is a clear indication that you are stepping out of your comfort zone. It is a normal reaction when we try something new and challenging. Yes, it can be scary to speak in public, but it is a viable way to grow your business and stay top-of-mind.

The good news is that you can overcome fear. Challenge yourself and make the decision to work on eliminating fear. Welcome the opportunity to experience new possibilities. Be firm in this resolution. Don't let fear stop you from getting more clients and becoming known in your niche by speaking. You can't move forward and be famous for your expertise if you stay where you are.

Have you ever heard fear described as False Evidence Appearing Real? Fear is a matter of perception. It doesn't matter if what you believe is true or false. If you attach a fearful thought to something, it becomes true for you. Your mind will feed you fear-based thoughts. It is normal. It will keep you from moving forward. Acknowledge this, but don't let it stop you. Change any negative, fear-based words that you currently use to positive statements. When you think about giving a talk, include words like fun, confident, empowered, engaging, exciting, and profitable. Visualize the outcome these words create in your mind. Enjoy the feeling conjured by the thoughts.

Visualize giving your speech. Create a mindset of confidence and competence even if you feel you aren't ready to star on stage. Picture the speech going well. What is the reaction you would like to see? Imagine it. Create a movie of it in your mind. Close your eyes and watch that movie over and over. Enjoy the experience. Feel the emotions in your body. The good news is that your mind does not distinguish between real and visualized performances. As a result, you will begin to radiate confidence, feel more relaxed and step into your power. Starting today, change your thoughts, visualize what you want, and feel the joy of receiving your desired result.

When you work through your fear, you drop the barrier between you and your audience. You suddenly stop thinking about yourself and start thinking about them. They will feel your engagement. By being fully present with your audience, they will connect with you in a positive way. The lady who broke out in red facial blotches focused on serving her audience. You need to do the same. You will receive the appreciation of your audience for making an authentic connection and delivering a message they came to hear.

When you step out of your comfort zone you are ready to play a bigger game. That is the step toward becoming known as an expert speaker.

Practice, Practice, Practice

Being prepared will help eliminate your fear. I don't believe in winging a speech. Delivering a good speech requires practice. If you care about your audience, you will show up prepared and ready to deliver an engaging presentation. The way to prepare is to rehearse. All stars rehearse so their performance will shine. They don't show up on stage or a movie set and make up their lines. They show up knowing their script and how they should deliver the content. You must do the same.

In order to control nervousness, become comfortable with your script. Rehearse your speech as often as possible to increase your familiarity with your content. Your goal is to feel comfortable saying the words and sharing your message. The confidence you gain while you practice will translate into a smoother, less stressful speech in front of a group.

Read your speech out loud when you practice. What looks good on paper doesn't always sound the same when spoken. You want to aim for a conversational tone. Don't deliver a monologue. Practice as if you are performing your speech. Include changes in tonality, pacing, and volume. Work on the transitions in your speech. Your points should flow seamlessly and not have jarring stops and starts. Will you use slides or props? If so, include them during your practice session so you become familiar handling them.

It is critical to time your presentation practice sessions. Design your talk to be under the amount of time you are given to speak. This allows for any unforeseen problems that may result including technical difficulties, interruptions and schedule changes. You never want to go over the time given for a speech. The organizers will not be pleased if you disrupt the schedule. You run the risk of not being asked to speak to the organization in the future. Your audience will also notice if your speech runs long. You don't want them to start looking at their watches and tune you out. For these reasons, practicing your timing is critical to the success of your speech.

Don't read your script to your audience. It gives the impression that you are unsure of your material. If you are nervous or afraid of forgetting what you will say, make notes that you can refer to. Create visuals on slides that will trigger cues as you speak. Adequate practice will help you feel comfortable with your talk. Each time you speak, it will get easier. In Chapter 8 you will learn effective ways to create visuals for your presentation.

Production houses sometimes offer sneak previews before the launch of a new movie. You can do the same by practicing in front of people you are comfortable being with. Invite your close friends and family members to preview your speech. Ask for feedback and try incorporating the suggestions you receive. You'll quickly discover whether your audience is engaged, understands your key points, or has lots of clarifying questions.

A big key to overcoming fear is being ready, prepared and focused on the content you will deliver. When you know your material and have a solid understanding of your message you will be able to communicate your key points, control any nervousness, and make transitions seamlessly. With preparation your unique self can be center stage and in the spotlight.

My husband and I are competitive ballroom dancers. The amount of practice needed to be able to compete and outshine our competition is staggering. If you are wondering how often we take lessons and practice, the answer is almost every day. We have a dance room in our house. When we aren't out practicing and dancing, we do it at home. We never step out on a competition floor without many hours of practice and preparation. I use this same approach when I speak. Being nervous is normal, but I practice and prepare so that I can stand in the spotlight.

Controlling Fear

Breathing is key when it comes to speaking. When we are nervous we tend to hold our breath. Good breathing will help control your nervousness and give your voice better resonance. Breathing can calm you, center you, and relax your mind.

The first thing you should do before going out on stage is to focus on your breath. Breathing before taking the stage can help get nerves under control. Find a space to sit quietly and breathe.

Take a deep breath in and hold it for a few seconds. Breathe out with the sound "Ahhhhhh." Do this several times to release your nervous energy.

There are exercises and relaxation techniques you can employ to calm you before your performance. Roll your shoulders forward and back. Stretch your body to loosen your muscles. This will increase relaxation and blood flow throughout your body. Take some time to open and close your mouth by stretching your jaw. Some speakers find humming is a good way to warm up their vocal cords. You can also recite poetry, simple rhymes, or have fun with tongue twisters. These warm-up techniques will reduce your stress and prepare you vocally.

Another technique is grounding. Grounding exercises will center you, drive your energy into your feet, and help you be fully present. You want to use grounding techniques on stage. To do this, walk onstage and stand with your feet slightly apart. Ground yourself by creating energy down your legs and into the floor. It will prevent you from swaying, escalate your confidence, and enable you to connect with your audience by being fully present. The audience wants to engage with a self assured speaker.

Don't stand with your feet close together, or cross one foot in front of the other. Women tend to do this. It results in making women look small and prevents them from having a strong presence with the audience. Not standing properly can also throw you off balance. Men don't tend to do this. They know how to take space with their bodies when they are seated or standing. This is an important stage skill.

When you arrive onstage, walk confidently to the center front section and ground your energy into the floor. Don't rush to start speaking. Use this moment to look at your audience and visually connect with them. When you have their attention and they feel your presence, you are ready to begin speaking.

If you start to feel nervous and notice that you are accelerating your speaking speed, take a breath. Focused breathing will calm you and help slow your rate of speech.

Someone once shared this tip with me – if your mouth gets dry when speaking and you don't have water, bite your tongue. It increases saliva in your mouth. It works, but I don't like the look. For that reason I remember to keep a bottle of water nearby. Make sure your water is room temperature. Cold water can constrict your throat. I find a constant need to clear my throat if I drink ice water. Don't make this discovery during your speech.

Your Authentic Voice

Relax. You don't need to put on an act and try to impress anyone. You're the one the audience wants to see and hear. When you speak from your heart you will create the strongest connection with your audience. Your authentic voice and message will set you apart from all other speakers. Be yourself. Don't act or try to be someone you're not. Share what makes you unique. You will own the stage when you own your message.

Stage Presence

Step into your confidence when you step onto the stage. When you have stage presence you connect with your audience. Speak to the group as though you were speaking to one person. If you start to feel less confident and experience some fear or nervousness, just fake it until you make it. Act as if you are already a little bit famous. An actor takes on the role of the character they are portraying and you should do the same. Feel confident, and soon you will be.

Earlier I described the amount of practice my husband and I do when preparing for ballroom competitions. Part of our training includes how you walk onto a competition dance floor. The man offers his arm to his lady, the lady accepts, and the couple walks swiftly onto the floor to claim their spot. There will be many couples entering the floor at the same time. Spots are not given to you. The goal is to go get the best floor position possible. Posture is critical. You hold yourself with the look of a champion and show the judges that you are a competitor.

Couples don't look at their competition, they just claim their space on the floor. It doesn't matter if they are nervous. It doesn't matter if they feel others are stronger dancers. Competitors act as if they are champions. The more competitions a dancer enters, the more they feel and perform like a champion. Think of speaking as entering a dance floor and performing in a competition.

Once you step onto the stage, move front and center. This is your starting point, but, like a dancer that moves around the entire dance floor, I encourage you to use the entire stage.

Think of the movement in a play, or dancers doing a performance. It would be less exciting to watch performers if they stood in one place. Use the space strategically. I like to walk to a spot and make a point. When I want to go back to a point, I strategically walk back to the spot where I originally made the point I want to reinforce. You can also point to the spot where the point was made. It creates a visual for your audience.

You can also use the stage as a timeline. Walk to your right when speaking about the past. Visually this is left for your audience. Move up the timeline to your left, their right, as you tell stories that move forward in time. You can walk back or point to the appropriate spot on the floor when you what to revisit a point previously made.

I don't believe in scripting all of your movements as you want to be natural, however it makes sense to use movements that drive home your points. This will become easier, the more you speak. Keep in mind that there is balance in movement. You don't want to be a statue or, at the other extreme, a pacer. These fight or flight actions result from being nervous. Look to your feet for cues. If you notice you are moving non-stop, or not moving at all, calm yourself by breathing and ground your energy.

Are you familiar with a television show called *Dog Whisperer*? People who had dogs with behavior problems would contact Caesar Milan, the Dog Whisperer, to help them correct the behavior of their dog.

In one episode a couple could not get their dog to go outside and walk on a leash. The dog was terrified and would put out his paws and pull back trying to stop the outdoor walk. The owners, not knowing what to do, would gently drag the dog outside to the grass. This happened every day. In desperation the couple called Caesar Milan and asked for his help.

Caesar went to their home, watched the dog's behavior, and in his amazing way, knew exactly what to do. He tied a string to the dog's tail. Raising the string in one hand, and holding the leash in the other, he took the dog for a walk. At first, the dog was tentative, but within moments he was walking outside. We soon see this dog strutting his stuff. He's proud. He's walking in the neighborhood. He's acknowledging other animals and people. When a dog's tail is up, he's confident. The owners could not believe what they saw. Eventually the dog didn't need the string on his tail. He stepped into his confidence.

When you step on stage, put an imaginary string on your confidence. Wag your symbolic tail. I want you to fake it until you make it. Before you know it, you will believe in yourself and have a strong presence on stage.

KEY POINTS TO REMEMBER

• It's normal to get butterflies when getting up on stage.

• Your presentation is about your audience. It's not about you.

• Focus on the fact that giving a speech is about sharing information.

• When you work through your fear, you drop the barrier between you and your audience.

• Being prepared will help eliminate fear.

• Practice, practice, practice.

• Read your speech out loud when you practice.

• Time your practice sessions.

• Design your talk to be under the amount of time allotted.

• Don't read your script to your audience.

• Make notes that you can refer to.

• Breathing is key when it comes to speaking.

• Keep a bottle of room temperature water nearby.

• Be yourself. Don't act or try to be someone you're not.

• Don't be a statue or a pacer.

• Fight or flight actions result from being nervous.

• Be aware of your movements on stage.

• Fake it until you make it.

• If your mouth gets dry when speaking, bite your tongue to increase saliva in your mouth.

ACTION ITEMS

• Challenge yourself and make the decision to eliminate fear and experience new possibilities.

• Change negative, fear-based words that you currently use to positive statements.

• Create a mindset of confidence and competence even if you feel you aren't ready to star on stage.

• Practice in front of people you are comfortable being with. Ask for feedback.

• Before taking the stage take a deep breath in, hold it for a few seconds, then breathe out with the sound "Ahhhhhh." Do this several times to release your nervous energy.

• Before giving a speech, stretch your body to loosen your muscles and warm up your vocal cords.

• Ground yourself by creating energy into the floor.

CHAPTER 4
RED CARPET READY

I went to hear a speaker give a talk on a topic that I thought would be beneficial. I heard little of what the speaker delivered. Visually she distracted me.

Her outfit was so disconnected to her message that I kept looking at her attire. She wore an array of colors and ill fitting clothes. Her too short pants showcased her ankles and emphasized her scuffed shoes. A multi-colored jacket was covered in pins; her hair was piled strangely on top of her head with pieces hanging down, and every time she moved her hands there was a display of rings that encircled many fingers.

My mind was filled with my own thoughts, leaving little room for her content.

Your Image

Appearances are important. People will judge you within seconds of seeing you for the first time. Don't miss the opportunity to get an audience to buy into your message by distracting them with your appearance.

How do you know if your image is in alignment with your message? Start with a critical self-assessment.

Look in a full length mirror and answer the following questions:

Do you like what you see?

Will you make the best or worst dressed list?

Does your image match the way you want to look?

Does your image represent who you are?

What do people respond to when they look at you?

If you could change one thing, what would it be?

What do you like the best?

How you dress impacts how you present yourself and how you are perceived. You need to look the part you want to play. It's time to create your celebrity brand.

A speaker must have a powerful image because it is the basis of a first impression. Your look should express your personality. Create a public image that resonates with you. How do you want to stand out and differentiate yourself from your competition?

Your image matters wherever you go. Beyond speaking engagements, you will be making other appearances. You will be seen at networking events, meetings, and social gatherings. Your image is visible every time you are out in public. Be consistent with your brand image from the moment you arrive at a venue until the moment you leave. Don't fade into the background. Create a look that is memorable and appropriate for your message and your audience. Consistently promote your look on your marketing materials. Your goal is to carry your image through in everything you do.

Wardrobe

Dress the part you want to represent. Tailoring is

critical. Your clothes must fit properly. If you are going to use a clip-on microphone, make sure you are wearing clothes that easily allow you to attach the clip.

If you are in a situation where you are required to stay behind the lectern, you will have all the focus on your face. Wear an attractive color near your face and have a flattering hairdo. The color of your clothing needs to make you look your best and work with your skin tone and hair color. Don't convince yourself that your clothing is right when you feel uncertain. If it doesn't serve you, don't wear it.

You must be comfortable in your clothing choices. Select fabrics that don't easily wrinkle. Avoid fabrics that can make noise with your movements. For example, when legs brush together when wearing corduroy, a swishing sound might be heard. Shoes should be in style with your wardrobe. Don't sacrifice comfort when it comes to shoes. When you are speaking, you will be standing on your feet. You don't want your feet to hurt. Your movements on stage can become stilted without your knowing it.

After you dress the part, be mindful of your posture. Stand tall and try not to slouch. Pull your shoulders back and down. Raise your chin so that you are looking straight ahead. Make eye contact with your audience. Good posture has the benefit of helping you look confident on stage while giving your voice better resonance.

Accessories

The key to stretching your wardrobe, without stretching your wardrobe dollars, is accessorizing. Adding jewelry can totally change the look and feel of an outfit. It has the special ability to help you define your personal style and express who you are. It's the secret ingredient that women and men use to take their wardrobe from ho hum to wow.

The size of your jewelry is important. Small necklaces will not be seen from the stage. Women, you want to draw attention to your face with power necklaces. You should buy necklaces that are bold statement pieces that truly make an outfit have impact. These pieces make heads turn and adds the wow factor every time.

Look at the pictures of your favorite celebrities on the red carpet. What are they wearing that catches your eye? If you're drawn to a statement necklace, wear it and watch the reaction you get.

Celebrities know how to make a wow statement. Try a bold necklace and see for yourself. You'll be stepping into your own style.

Earrings are a marvelous finishing accessory for an outfit. Silver, gold, cubic zirconia, crystals, gemstones, and diamonds can add sparkle to your face.

Rings draw attention to our hands and can make a quiet or bold statement when worn on stage. Many people wear a ring that sparkles, as it keeps attention on the speaker.

Men, if it fits your style, you can also experiment with jewelry. Speaker Larry Winget uses rings and earrings to his advantage. They play a key role in creating his brand image.

Explore different options and see how the colors and metals look with your skin tone and wardrobe selections. The key to finding your jewelry style is to experiment with different looks. Use your imagination as you mix and match your favorite pieces.

I want to offer a word of caution on noisy accessories. Don't wear jangly bracelets. Bracelets are a wonderful way to add versatility to your look. Many people love to layer bracelets, but the movement of bracelets on your arm can be distracting. Bangles can also create noise as they slide into each other. When it comes to bracelets, wear only one on your wrist to finish your look, or skip it altogether.

Necklaces should not come in contact with your clip-on microphone. Plan your accessories with this in mind. The noise will be noticeable and you will have a constant need to adjust your jewelry.

Noise is not limited to accessories. Men, if you have coins in your pocket, remove them before your speech to prevent jiggling the coins during your talk. Trust me, the noise will be a distraction.

On a separate note, hand motions are welcome during a speech, but putting your hands in your pockets is not one of them.

Attitude

Your brand creates a positive attitude, which I consider to be a major accessory! When you exude confidence, people will magnetically be drawn to you. When you have an engaging personality, a smile on your face, and a desire to help others with your message, people will want to be around you and hear what you have to say. Let your positive attitude shine through in all that you do.

Hair

Now that you are creating your own celebrity brand, you need a hairdo that will help you look like a star. If you can't manage a complicated style, keep hair simple. Your hairstyle should match the image you want to portray. Your hairstyle should also match the formality or casualness of your clothing choices. The key point to keep in mind is that your hair should be presentable and in keeping with the look you want to communicate.

Makeup

Women, the point of using makeup will most likely resonate with you. Men, you should consider makeup if you are speaking on television. The goal is to be ready for your close up. It is an extension of looking appropriate for the occasion.

If you are on stage under bright lights, you will be washed out if you do not use makeup. Analyze the situation where you will be speaking and use makeup accordingly. The more intense the lighting, the greater the need for makeup.

Photos

Be consistent in presenting your look to the public. You should use the same image on your Website, Bio, About You Page, Speaker's One Sheet, Social Media Images, and Marketing Materials.

Your pictures should tell your story and capture your essence. A headshot is a closeup photo about you, not your surroundings. You are the star. Have a professional, clear, well-lit photo where the focus is on your face.

Create paparazzi moments. When you do speaking engagements, take pictures with your fans and feature them on your website and company newsletter. Your fans will love that you care enough to showcase being with them.

Keep your photos updated every few years so that they always look like you. You don't want people to come hear you speak and not be able to pick you out of the crowd. If you use video, it is particularly important that your photo image be consistent with your video image.

Video

All the world's a stage, especially now that video is

a popular internet medium. If you use your own website videos or have a YouTube channel, it is very important to keep a branded, consistent image in the way you deliver your message. Let people feel like they know you when they watch your videos.

If you are able to videotape your speeches, place video clips on your website. People that book speakers watch video clips to screen potential speakers.

One Sheet

A One Sheet is the speaker's version of an actor's Headshot. It should include your bio, testimonials, information on the topic you speak about, and a photo or two of you. One photo can be a headshot and one can be an action shot.

The One Sheet should have the same branded look and feel as the other marketing materials in your speaker's kit. The One Sheet is your calling card into the speaking world. Make it memorable.

KEY POINTS TO REMEMBER

• People judge you within seconds of seeing you for the first time.

• Create a look that is memorable and appropriate for your message and your audience.

• Carry your image through in everything you do.

• Dress appropriately and be mindful of your posture.

• Accessories can help define your personal style and express who you are.

• Do not wear items that will make noise on stage and distract from your speech.

• Your hair should be presentable and in keeping with the style you want to communicate.

• The more intense the lighting, the greater the need for makeup.

• Your pictures should tell your story and capture your essence.

• Be memorable.

ACTION ITEMS

• Exude confidence and people will be drawn to you.

• If you are able to videotape your speeches, place video clips on your website.

• Create a One Sheet that includes your bio, testimonials, information on the topic you speak about, and a photo or two of you.

ACT 2: PRESENT

CHAPTER 5
SHOWTIME

Two couples that I am friends with in the United States were excited to tour Europe. They were eager to set off on the vacation of a lifetime.

The woman, whom I will call Jane, must have the bladder the size of a pea. Fearful that she would always be hours from a restroom, she stopped at every bathroom she encountered.

One day she approached a restroom that was coin operated. She put the required coin in, turned the knob, and opened the door. She took one look inside and promptly decided that she could not enter. As she turned away the door began to close. My friend, whom I will call John, sprang forward and grabbed the closing door. "If you're not going to use it, I might as well go in."

John stepped inside and prepared to use the facilities. As he did so the toilet began to move. He endeavored to keep up with it. Then the lights went out. He persisted. Soon the water sprinklers turned on. There was no turning back now. When Jane allowed the door to start closing, the restroom went into cleaning mode!

Eventually everything in the restroom went back to normal and John opened the door and stepped outside. His three companions stared at him in disbelief. He came out soaking wet. John looked at them and said, "I think I went to the bathroom in a car wash!" John's friends still laugh uncontrollably every time they tell the "car wash" story.

My takeaway: know what you are heading into ahead of time!

Arrive Early

No one likes surprises. As a speaker you want to be as prepared as possible before you take the stage. My best advice is to get to your engagement early. Visit the room where you will speak and check the equipment you will use. Give yourself time to familiarize yourself with the setup and make any changes necessary.

I remember one of the first speeches I gave to an association. None of the computer connections were compatible with my laptop and the flash drive wouldn't work. I tried emailing my presentation to the organizer, but couldn't get internet access. I didn't think to send my presentation before my arrival. I eventually gave up on technology. As I was very rehearsed, I was able to give my presentation without the use of slides. Those hours of practice paid off! The audience was none the wiser. You never know what you will encounter, so arrive early and get the lay of the land.

After seeing the room and checking the audio and visual hookups, interact and network with the attendees. Talk to as many as possible and learn their names. When people make a connection with you, they will feel like they know you when you are speaking. You can even refer to things that audience members said to you during the networking session, if it relates directly to your speech and doesn't make anyone feel uncomfortable.

Lights, Camera, Action

Write out your introduction before hand and give it to the person who will be introducing you. Do not leave this to chance. Thoughtfully craft what you want to say. Try to reinforce for the audience the message you want to be known for. Keep it brief and don't go on and on about your credentials unless you are giving an academic talk, or addressing an audience where your professional background is key.

Before you know it, it will be time for your introduction. Try to get to the stage while the applause is still going on. This gives you momentum and a strong connection with the audience from the start.

Whenever possible take center stage. Don't stand behind the lectern. You don't want to put a barrier between you and your audience. You want to be as close to them as possible. Visually take in the audience. Smile. You don't have to start speaking immediately.

This is going to sit uncomfortably with some of you, but it needs to be told. Don't start by thanking your audience and don't start by thanking your organizer. The goal is to capture the attention of the audience in the first 10 seconds or risk losing them before your speech begins. You want to grab attention in such a way that you bring them out of their own heads and have them focus on you, the speaker.

So how do you make the best use of those first moments? You start with a strong opening. This is critical as it sets the stage for your talk. Your opening can tell a startling fact, a relevant statistic, a thought provoking statement, or if you're good at it, you can try humor. If you are not good at humor, it is best not to use this method. Another powerful opening is to start with a story. People love stories because they become emotionally involved in the message.

A story visually creates a scene an audience can immerse themselves in. Let your words paint a picture that moves your listeners to the edge of their seats and has them wanting to hear more. Through stories, you will engage your audience by activating their imagination. The key is to arouse their interest with a story that relates to the topic of your talk. We will discuss this in detail in the section on storytelling.

Your opening needs to be strong. I always think of the song *"You Had Me From Hello"* by

Kenny Chesney. Remember this title when you sit down and write the opening statement for your next speech.

If you want to thank your organizer, do so after your strong opening.

Know Your Opening Lines

The opening is so important that you should never leave it to chance. You do not need to memorize your entire presentation, but I encourage you to memorize the opening to your speech. When you start to speak, your goal is to get your audience interested and involved in what you are saying. A well written and delivered opening makes all the difference between an audience that tunes in and one that tunes out.

I had the opportunity to work with a young client, whom I'll call Lisa. She was representing her high school in a speech competition. Lisa told me that her speech was on the topic of mindset. I listened to her speech, but she didn't bring me to the edge of my seat. Lisa spoke about taking care of the weeds that grew in the garden of her mind. She spoke about thinking positive thoughts and keeping negative thoughts at bay. The speech was one that I heard many times before. It was a good analogy, but it wasn't original and it didn't have the conviction it should have.

Gently I asked, "Lisa, is there something that ever occurred in your life, that relates to mindset, that you can personally share with the audience?" I was looking for her to make a deeper connection with her audience. She pondered this for a short time and told me that she couldn't think of anything.

I walked her to her car and while we were walking I mentioned that I saw an Oprah episode where Tony Robbins had Oprah walk on fire. Without hesitating Lisa said, "Oh, I walked on fire too." I stared at her as my jaw dropped. "You walked on fire?" I couldn't believe what I just heard. No matter how I thought about it, walking on fire wasn't something I wanted to try. It was a topic I wanted to hear more about.

Lisa explained how she went to a Tony Robbins weekend and how he prepared her mind to accept the fact that she could walk on fire and not get burned. "That's your mindset story," I excitedly told her. She looked at me in silence, not believing that it was a good story. I asked her, "How many people do you know that have walked on fire? People will be very interested in how you accomplished that."

Lisa re-worked her speech. On the day of the speech competition, Lisa walked out on stage, looked at her audience, paused, then said, "Mindset is everything. Do you know how I know? I walked on fire." She brought her audience to the edge of their seats. They fully focused their attention on what she had to say.

Although Lisa missed placing for nationals by one spot, she learned the value of getting the immediate attention of her audience by having a strong opening statement. Lisa now uses this skill when preparing for all her speech competitions.

How can you open your speech to get your audience yearning for more?

KEY POINTS TO REMEMBER

• Before your speech, visit the room where you will speak and check the equipment that you will use.

• Prior to your speech, network with the attendees. They will feel like they know you when you are speaking.

• Get to the stage while the applause is still going on and use the momentum to make a strong connection with the audience from the start.

• When possible, don't stand behind the lectern as you don't want a barrier between you and your audience.

• Don't start your speech by thanking your audience or the organizer.

• Capture the attention of the audience in the first 10 seconds or you'll risk losing them before your speech begins.

• A strong opening can utilize a startling fact, a relevant statistic, a thought provoking statement, humor, or a story.

ACTION ITEMS

• Create a strong opening to your speech that has your audience yearning to know more.

• Memorize the opening to your speech and don't leave it to chance.

CHAPTER 6
RED HOT PRESENTATIONS

I will always remember my early days when I struggled to break out of my world of silence. Finding my voice gave me the opportunity to soar. It fueled me to reach new heights and bring attention to the contributions I could offer the world.

Empowered by the gift of speech and my love of acting, I contacted an Executive Producer of a television talk show. I pitched an idea for a consumer series. I spoke and she listened. My pitch was on how supermarket shoppers could get paid to buy food for their families. I had her interest. She told me, "Come in and meet with me. I want to interview you in person. If you are good, I'll give you one show, if you are great, I'll give you a series."

With great excitement and anticipation I prepared for my interview. I put together ideas and visuals for a series. I created show ideas with enticing hooks to keep the audience wanting to see more each day. The producer loved my ideas and I landed the series.

The shows generated carloads of mail. I made many trips to the television studio to fill my car with the fan mail I received. The television show positioned me as an expert in my niche. It brought me opportunities to appear on other television shows and radio.

I secured the series because the Executive Producer clearly understood what I would tell the television audience and the benefit the viewers would receive.

Coming Attractions

After your strong opening, it is time to transition into the body of your speech. Start with the coming attractions. Pull back the curtain and tell your audience what they are going to learn as a result of your talk.

In the body of your speech you discuss the key points you want your audience to remember. Draw your listeners in with information they want to know. Every speech should have a main theme that is broken down into specific speaking points that you will explain. Think of it as a roadmap detailing the verbal journey you will share with your audience. I tell my audience that I will share my 3 P's of Presenting: Prepare, Present and Profit, the same 3 P's that I am expanding upon in this book.

Connect with your audience

It's critically important not to bore your audience. You will make the strongest connection when you use your authentic voice. Have passion about the message you share and speak from your heart. When you do, you will create engagement with your audience throughout your talk. Avoid giving a flat unemotional speech.

Please keep in mind that the speech you are delivering is not about you. It's about your audience. The audience is waiting to hear a message that relates to them. As a speaker you need to address the question, "What does my audience want to hear?" Take this question seriously and give it the research it deserves. By answering the question, you will deliver relevant information.

Throughout your speech you want to evoke a feeling of connection. Even though you are speaking to a room full of people, make each person feel as though you are speaking only to him or her. Smile at your audience, use eye contact, and create interaction. The more involved an audience is, the more likely they will remember you. Your goal is to become the top-of-mind expert in your field.

Think of the movies and television shows that you like to watch. There are so many different ways to deliver entertainment. There are drama, comedy, and suspense to name a few. Here are some trigger questions to help you think of ways to engage your audience.

How can you create drama for your audience and draw them in?

How can you use humor and make them laugh?

How can you build suspense in your stories and have them wanting to know more?

Can you include interactive exercises to involve the audience?

When I give a speech and want to drive home the point about connecting with the audience, I have a game where I am a mind reader and demonstrate that I know what my audience is thinking. My mind reading game is fun, interactive and memorable. Show your audience a good time. Many times your next speaking opportunity will come from someone in your audience. This is your moment to showcase audience engagement. You never know who in the audience can help you become well-known for what you do.

Delivery

As a speaker, your voice is your greatest asset. How you use your vocal instrument will ultimately determine your connection with your audience. Pacing and pausing is important. You don't want to rush through your speech, nor do you want to speak too slowly. Your rate of speech should speed up and slow down like a piece of music. Vary the tempo. Volume is also critical. Though you want to be heard, don't shout at your audience or speak too softly. Place special emphasis on the words you want to draw attention to. Allow these key points to determine your volume. I once attended a talk where I could barely hear the speaker. I felt as if I were eavesdropping on a private conversation. It was a struggle to stay engaged.

The tone of your voice is equally important. Vary your tone to prevent sounding monotone. Use of inflection will add drama to your speech. Variety of sounds creates vocal interest.

Modulate your pitch to convey emotion. Your pitch should go up when you want the audience to get excited and down when you want them to think about what you said. You don't want to continuously speak in a high pitch. Women, this is more true for you than it is for men. Remember to drop your voice down at the end of a sentence. If you raise your voice up, it will sound like you are asking a question. It will make you sound unsure of the information you are delivering.

Diction is an important part of communicating as well. Be careful not to slur your words or pronounce words incorrectly. Aim for clarity in your speech. If you have a regional dialect and you are speaking outside of your geographic area, practice enunciating clearly so that the audience understands your message.

Practice your speech so that you eliminate the use of filler words. These include um, ah, er, eh, so, like, you know. If you tend to use filler words, become aware of when you use them and practice speaking without them. When practicing your speech have someone help you become aware of this tendency.

Filler words are often used because we are uncomfortable with silence and fill the void with sound while we think about what to say. Get comfortable with silence. When used appropriately, silence gives your audience time to reflect on your message. Strive to build in moments of silence.

Sometimes we also use filler words when speaking quickly. This happens when we forget to slow down and breathe. Don't rush your speech.

Show & Tell

People love visuals and tend to remember an image and props more than the spoken word. If you have items you can show during your speech, it will help your audience remember the point you are making.

My signature speech is about becoming famous in your niche by learning how to become a great speaker. My props include a replica of an Oscar Award statue to drive home the element of speaking fame, a movie clap board to state my name and own my area of expertise, a mirror to reinforce the importance of brand image, and other related items.

Using props will make your point come to life. We are visual creatures. When possible add images that relate to your talk and are memorable. Slides are a visual part of a presentation. For slides to be memorable they need to be created properly and used effectively. I will discuss the use of slides in Chapter 8.

Non-Verbal Messages

Don't distract from your speech by giving the wrong message with your body language. Non-verbal messages are as important as verbal messages. Many times they speak louder than the spoken word.

What non-verbal messages are you delivering? If possible try to video yourself delivering a speech, or have someone give you feedback.

Are you smiling or do you look unapproachable and distant?

Are your arms crossed or are they relaxed and open?

Is your head down or are you making eye contact with your audience?

Is your back to the audience as you read your slides or are you speaking to your audience?

Are you visually distracted because you are thinking of what you need to say or are you clearly delivering your presentation?

Are you pacing because you are nervous or using the stage comfortably?

Non-verbal messages can be positive or negative. They can create audience engagement or they can stop people from listening. Try to be aware of your non-verbal actions. Your body language should reinforce the points you are trying to make.

KEY POINTS TO REMEMBER

• After your strong opening, transition into the body of your speech.

• Discuss the key points you want your audience to remember.

• Every speech should have a primary theme.

• Do not bore your audience. Evoke a feeling of connection.

• Smile at your audience, use eye contact, and create interaction.

• The more involved an audience is, the more likely they will remember you.

• How you use your voice will determine your connection with your audience.

• When used appropriately, silence gives your audience time to reflect on your message.

• People love visuals. Images and props will help your audience remember the point you are making.

• Don't distract from your speech by giving the wrong message with your body language.

ACTION ITEMS

• Address the question, "What does my audience want to hear?" When you answer the question, you will deliver relevant information.

• Think of an interactive exercise that you can use to involve your audience.

• Practice your speech so that you eliminate the use of filler words.

• Build moments of silence into your speech.

CHAPTER 7
SET THE SCENE

The curtain went up and I could hear an audible gasp. As I leaped onto the stage as Peter Pan, the children's eyes riveted on me. We traveled together on a journey into fantasyland. Slowly, invitingly, I brought them to the edge of their seats as I shared Peter's stories of adventure and feats of wonder.

Storytelling

People, young and old, have an emotional connection to stories. Our culture embraces storytelling. This can be seen in movies, sitcoms, commercials, the books we read, the conversations we share, the bedtime stories we tell our children.

Stories have created the fabric of legend and memories. We may not always take in messages when they are delivered as facts. We are more likely to understand information when placed in a story. A story creates an experience. The magic happens when facts come to life in our imaginations.

As a speaker, your listeners need to relate to what is being said and become emotionally involved. Share your personal story if you desire to create a buzz about yourself. It's how you'll be remembered. Talk about yourself in a way that draws people in and creates a longing to hear more. Don't be generic. Create your own character that ideally suits your personality and your values.

When you share your personal story it tells people who you are, why you do what you do, and why they should care. Use dialogue that will give your story your unique voice.

Conversation puts people in the scene. Start with your struggle so people can relate to your difficulties. Paint a picture of what you went through. Breathe life into your story. Transition to the moment that put you on a new path and started your transformation. Conclude with the happy ending that resulted in your success and what you now bring to the world.

Describe the characters in your story so that people can see them as you speak. When people are captivated by your story they will want to know more about what you do and how you do it. The outcome is that story creates connection. When you authentically share what you care about, it gives your message a voice that is yours alone. This is your starring role. Be the star in your own story, not a bit player or background extra. Your story tells people who you are and why they should care.

Your personal story is only one of the many stories you can share. You will arouse audience interest if you use different stories to drive home your message and key points. In your stories you can plant seeds of the benefits people receive by working with you.

Tell compelling stories that stir emotions and transports your audience into the scene. Let your stories recreate memories that take your listeners back in time.

Paint a picture with your words so that you create a visual movie in the mind of your listener. Use words involving the five senses during your speech. Let your audience hear, smell, taste, touch and see what you are sharing. The key is to use words that transport your listener into the scene.

Stimulate an array of emotional responses. I like to use the word "imagine" to create a picture of what I am saying because stories engage an audience by activating their imagination.

It is important that a speaker not tell the wrong story. The key is to arouse interest with a story that relates to the topic of your talk and is relevant to the content you are delivering. Drive your points home with strategic storytelling.

Do not interrupt the flow of your stories by asking questions of your audience. Keep the flow going until you are ready to transition.

You are a creator with your words. Allow your words to move an audience to the edge of their seats and create a desire within them that leaves them wanting to hear more.

KEY POINTS TO REMEMBER

• Your personal story tells people who you are, why you do what you do, and why they should care.

• Use dialogue. Conversation puts people in the scene in your story.

• Your personal story is only one of the many stories you can share.

• In your stories, plant seeds of the benefits people will receive by working with you.

• People are more likely to understand information that is placed in stories.

• Paint a picture with your words so that you create a visual movie in the mind of your listener.

• Drive your points home with strategic storytelling.

• Do not interrupt the flow of your stories by asking questions of your audience.

• Use stories to create a desire to hear more.

ACTION ITEMS

• Write your personal story.

• Create compelling stories that stir emotions.

• Use words in your stories that involve the five senses. Let your audience hear, smell, taste, touch and see what you are sharing.

CHAPTER 8
MOVIE CREDITS

Upon completion of his post-doctoral position at Harvard Medical School, my husband Jeff moved away from the academic world and walked toward his future as an inorganic chemist. He had invitations to apply to positions throughout the country. His travels took him to a chemical company, where he would interview for two long days.

At the end of day two, Jeff sat across from the personnel director to learn more about the scope of the position. The man started to drone on in a monotone. It was an endless stream of words. To make matters worse, the man started to look down at his feet. For an undetermined amount of time he spoke to his shoes. His voice slowly but surely lulled my husband to do the unthinkable. He fell asleep. I've never heard of anyone sleeping during a job interview, but Jeff assures me that it is true. He realized he had been asleep when his head suddenly fell forward and awakened him.

Realizing that he had been asleep, my husband sheepishly raised his eyes to look at the man behind the desk. Jeff couldn't believe what he saw. The man was still staring down, talking to his shoes in a monotone that would benefit insomniacs everywhere. The man cluelessly rambled on and on.

Eventually the monologue ended and, believe it or not, my husband was offered the position. Jeff politely declined.

Fast forward in time. The company where he interviewed is no longer in existence. The man that interviewed Jeff now has a chemistry lab down the hall from where my husband is employed. To this day the man doesn't know that Jeff fell asleep during the job interview.

My advice, don't bore your audience. Keep them engaged with your content. You don't want to risk putting your audience to sleep.

Don't Bore Your Audience

I know you have seen some yawn-inducing slide presentations, so I'm going to give you some red hot tips to dazzle your audience instead of putting them to sleep. Don't risk losing your audience by boring them. They'll never invest in doing business with you if they tune out too soon.

90% of what most people say in a presentation is forgotten soon after people leave the room. If you have information you need people to remember, create simple, yet powerfully visual slides and paint a picture with your words. PowerPoint can be very effective if used correctly. Your visual learners will sit up and say thank you.

Visuals

Do you read all the movie credits at the end of a movie? They can scroll on the screen for a long time. Most people exit after reading the names of the main characters. Do your slide presentations have this effect? Too much type and your audience may exit the theater physically or mentally.

A big tip is not to create your slides first.

Write your script first. Walk away from the urge to develop your content in PowerPoint. Create your presentation in Word, or on paper, and then use PowerPoint *after* you've structured your message. It will prevent you from overloading your slides with information. If you find you are losing the attention of your audience it means you've filled your slides with too many facts, slide after slide, forcing your audience to tune out.

The fewer bullets and words on your slides, the more the audience will listen to you. Think about the word "bullets" and remember that bullets are deadly. They facilitate Death by PowerPoint. Have you ever seen 15 bullet points on a slide? As an audience member you probably read all the information up on the screen. You finish reading the slide and the poor speaker is still on talking point number 3. Unfortunately, the agony doesn't stop there. The speaker clicks to the next slide and we see another 15 points! I don't know about you, but during such a presentation I start wondering how much longer I have to endure this agony. This is when an audience starts to tune out.

To make matters worse, there are the speakers that turn their back to their audience and read their slides. Don't read from your slides. Ever. You will lose your audience, even if you had them from hello. I coined a term for slide reading ad nauseam. I call it "Presentation Karaoke." Trust me, giving a presentation is not a karaoke event!

People can read faster than you can talk. If you are of a certain age, you may remember a television program called *Sing Along with Mitch*. The words to a song would appear on screen, and a little black dot would appear above the word that was being sung. Viewers were instructed to "follow the bouncing ball." Unless you want your audience to read out loud with you as you speak, don't read your slides.

Your narrative is the most important part of your PowerPoint. The slides just support what you are talking about. I'm not saying, don't ever use a bullet, but do it minimally. If you must use a bullet, never use a complete sentence.

Save all written bulleted information for a handout. And don't give out the handout while you're speaking. Distributing your material will have the same effect as having your information on your slides as people will start reading. Don't forget to put your contact information on your handout.

When there is information people need to

remember, create simple, yet powerfully visual slides and paint a picture with words. You can put a picture in a slide that visually explains what you want to say. Use an image that is fresh, creative and adds impact. The image should reinforce the point you are making in a memorable way.

Do not use colors that are hard to read, an array of fonts, and unnecessary animation. You don't want to distract your audience. You want your audience to look at you and listen to your message.

People like to ask me about charts. Charts and graphs should not command the audience's attention. You should. Let's say you have a chart that shows a 500% improvement in productivity over the past quarter. Just create a slide that says 500% and talk about the improvement.

Audience members spend too much time looking at charts and trying to figure out what they mean. And while they're doing that, they're not listening to you. But having 500% stand alone on a PowerPoint -- that's powerful. They'll remember that. That number will stay on the screen, as long as you talk about that topic. Save the chart for the handout.

Don't treat your speech as if it's a bedtime

story. You will only encourage snoring if you bore your audience. Keep your listeners engaged with your content. When you create your slides for your next speech, remember, your slides should not compete with you, the presenter. You are the star, not your slides.

KEY POINTS TO REMEMBER

• Don't bore your audience. Keep them engaged with your content.

• Too much type on a slide and your audience will tune out.

• Your narrative is the most important part of your PowerPoint.

• The fewer bullets and words on your slides, the more the audience will listen to you.

• If you use a bullet, never use a complete sentence.

• Don't read your slides.

• Distribute your handout after your speech.

• Put your contact information on your handout.

• Put a picture in a slide that visually explains what you want to say.

• On slides, do not use colors that are hard to read, an array of fonts, or unnecessary animation.

• Your slides should not compete with you, the speaker.

ACTION ITEMS

• Write your script before creating your PowerPoint slides.

• Don't develop your content in PowerPoint.

• Select memorable images that reinforce the points you want to make.

CHAPTER 9
QUESTIONS AND ANSWERS

When I was a young mother the little boy next door would come over and play with my son. The neighbor was an inquisitive child. He'd often say, "Scuze me, scuze me," and then proceed to ask me one question after the next. It was always entertaining to watch his train of thought.

Once, while I was in my backyard, I heard his voice through the bushes. He was asking his mother a string of questions. Each question was followed with "Why?" She would answer his question, but it only prompted another "Why?" Finally in exasperation I heard, "Because I'm your mother, that's why." The questions and answers had come to an end.

Handling Q&A

Sometimes it is easy for a speaker to answer audience questions, and sometimes questions can be a source of exasperation. The skill you exhibit when handling questions can make or break your speech.

This may surprise you, but don't take questions at the end of your speech. Questions asked after your prepared close can derail your presentation.

If you are giving a persuasive presentation, where you will be selling from the stage, hold the Q&A session before your call to action. If you are giving an educational talk, take questions before your close. During your speech, tell your audience to hold their questions and that you will answer questions before you wrap up. This informs people that they shouldn't interrupt you while you are speaking. It also states that your speech does not conclude after the Q&A.

I have seen speakers make the decision not to take questions during their speech. If that is your preference, state that you will not be taking questions but people can speak to you privately after your talk, by phone, by email, or however you want to approach it. If you are doing a full day speaking event, you may have times when people may line up and speak with you individually. Please provide clear instructions to your audience regarding Q&A because you don't want them to feel that you were unapproachable.

There are a few things to keep in mind in order to have a successful Q&A session. Part of preparing for your talk is to think of questions that might be asked. Write out brief succinct answers. When rehearsing your speech, include time to rehearse your questions and answers. When answering questions always refer back to points you want to drive home in your speech.

Even with the best preparation, it is possible for someone to ask a question you don't know the answer to. If that happens, be honest with your audience. Tell them you do not know the answer, but you would be happy to research it and share the information with the group by email. If the emails are not provided to you, offer to supply the information to the group organizer for distribution. Sometimes someone in the audience may volunteer the answer for the group. If that happens thank the person for sharing the information.

When you open the room for Q&A, state that

you have time to take three or four questions. If there are many hands raised for questions, offer to do a follow up teleseminar (group phone call) where you will answer additional questions. It is important to be aware of the amount of time you have remaining for your speech.

When people raise their hands, be cognizant to take questions from all parts of the room. As people, we have a natural inclination to look in certain directions. Be mindful of this and include all sections of your audience.

When someone asks a question, repeat the question so everyone can hear it. In some instances there are microphones that people can approach to ask a question, or you might have a runner that hands people a microphone. This will probably not be the case for most speeches that you will give, so repeat the question after it is asked.

Your goal is to create audience involvement and engagement. You will encourage questions when you make audience members feel good about their contribution. Remember, the speech is about them even during the Q&A session. If someone is asking a question, odds are others in the audience have the same question. Thank the person and acknowledge that they asked a good question.

On the off chance that you get a heckler in the audience, my best advice is to stay calm and focused. If you don't agree with something they've said, don't get into an argument. Try to give a neutral answer that doesn't derail the points you have been driving home in your speech. There are some people that need attention. Tell them you would be happy to talk with them privately. Move on and take another question as soon as possible.

As you end your Q&A session, tell your audience that they can connect with you after your speech if they have further questions.

KEY POINTS TO REMEMBER

• The skill you exhibit when handling questions can make or break your speech.

• Don't take questions at the end of your speech. Take questions before your close.

• Questions asked after your prepared close can derail your presentation.

• You can make the decision not to take questions during your speech.

• When answering questions refer back to points you want to drive home.

• If you do not know an answer to a question, be honest with your audience. Tell the audience you will research the question and communicate the answer.

• Take questions from all parts of the room.

• When someone asks a question, repeat the question so everyone can hear it.

• Make your audience feel good about their contribution by thanking them for their question.

• If you get a heckler in the audience, stay calm and focused. Give a neutral answer that doesn't derail the points you have been driving home in your speech.

• Tell your audience that they can connect with you after your speech if they have further questions.

ACTION ITEMS

• Think of questions that might be asked during your Q&A session.

• Write out brief succinct answers to possible questions.

• When practicing, include time to rehearse your answers.

ACT 3: PROFIT

CHAPTER 10
SELLING FROM THE STAGE

I admit it. I loved the singing sensation group *The Monkees*. They popped onto the music scene in 1966 and transformed my world. I was just starting junior high school. I was young and enthralled. I personally believe I was their biggest fan, though my girlfriends at the time would probably argue that they were. I bought every single record and album *The Monkees* produced, sang their songs until I was hoarse, and watched every episode of their television show. My bedroom was covered in pictures carefully cut from the magazine pages of *16 Magazine* and *Tiger Beat*. I was surrounded by Davy Jones, Micky Dolenz, Peter Tork and Michael Nesmith. I admit to having a huge crush on Micky.

My friends consoled me when he married. They knew my pain. Ah, the life of a fan.

Fan Club

How do you become a top-of-mind sensation? Start by creating a movement. You need to use the techniques discussed throughout this book. You need to share your authentic voice, and establish your brand.

What's your message?

What do you stand for?

What are you passionate about?

Why do you do what you do?

Respond to these questions and embody the answers. People will connect with you when, and only when, your message resonates with them. Don't just talk about what you do. Live, breathe and be what you represent and want to be known for. Let people relate to you and your cause.

To create a fan base, your goal can't be to reach everyone. As hard as it is to believe, not everyone loved *The Monkees* the way I did. Yes, it's true. Some people like pop music, some like rock and roll, others like folk songs. You can't be known for all things to all people.

Be yourself and share your gifts by speaking *your* message. You will reach the people who are in alignment with what you have to say. This is how you will grow a fan base. When you share your beliefs, your fans will speak of you to others and spread your message. What are your fans saying? Place their testimonials, your rave reviews, on your website. Invite them to endorse your work at select times during your talk. Let your fans sing your praises to the world.

Opportunities can appear when you impact people with your message.

Making An Offer

During your speech, your audience must believe you are providing valuable content. This is imperative if you plan to make an offer. When you provide content that is relevant and matters to your audience, they will be open to hearing your sales offer. They not only need to like your message, but they must feel a connection with you. Your goal is to create fans and entice people to take action to go further with you. Your fans will invest in your coaching or mastermind programs, or take you home with them in the form of your books, audio programs, DVDs, online courses, or however you package your expertise.

When you are a red hot presenter, you need to sell the sizzle. Tell your audience the benefit of working with you. Explain that in a short talk there is no way you can address all the steps they need to know. You don't want to give your audience so much content during your talk that they think they don't need further advice from you.

During your presentation give them the what and the why and some of the how. Your goal is to sell the rest of the how. Speak to the problem you will solve when they have the opportunity to work with you. They must believe that you have the solution to help them move forward quickly. You don't want to go into sales mode. You want to paint a picture of the transformation that other clients have experienced, why they needed your service, and the result past clients achieved. Let your listeners envision what is possible for them.

You can ask your audience what they feel was the most valuable content you shared in your speech. What they say is a step toward what they'll buy. It also gives confirmation to the entire group that your expertise is valued.

Talk to the emotions, the pain or the fear that your audience has and how you can help them overcome the situation.

Create a strong desire before you make your offer. A technique that is effective is to have a drawing for a product you are selling. It makes the people in the audience want to have it. You are setting the stage for back of room sales.

You want to seed the picture of transformation and what is possible for your audience throughout your speech. Tell them why you offer what you offer. Your call to action drives home the ability to finally solve their problem. Your entire talk brings you to this moment. Making an offer is your commercial or infomercial. It is critical that it be well scripted. You do not want to leave the wording to chance.

When you create a call to action you must be very clear in terms of what you want your audience to do. When people have too many choices they get confused and don't move forward. You want to create action by having a single offer that resonates with them. It must be something they want so badly they are willing to pay for it and won't go home without your necessary product or service. You are offering what they have been searching for.

Once you make your offer, keep moving them toward making a decision. Hand out the order form and have one in your hand. Tell them exactly how the form should be completed. Have a fast acting bonus that includes extra goodies for the first X number of people that buy today. You can pick any number that works for you. You can also have "today only" pricing. You want to create urgency because the chance for a sale greatly decreases once they leave the room. State a risk-free guarantee that takes away the fear of purchase.

A well-crafted speech can result in a high sales volume. It is your opportunity to work further with people who need the services you provide in your area of expertise. If you want to make a name for yourself, become top-of-mind and increase your client base, you need to cultivate raving fans. It may very well put you on the road to fame and fortune.

KEY POINTS TO REMEMBER

• People will connect with you when your message resonates with them.

• Your fans will sing your praises to the world.

• Provide valuable content during your speech.

• Fans will invest in your products and services.

• Tell your audience the benefit of working with you. Speak to the problem you will solve.

• Create a strong desire before making your offer.

• Ask your audience what they feel was the most valuable content you shared. What they say is a step toward what they'll buy.

• Create a call to action by having a single offer that resonates with your audience.

• Keep moving your audience toward a decision.

• Create urgency because once people leave the room the chance for a sale greatly decreases.

• Raving fans can put you on the road to fame and fortune.

ACTION ITEMS

• Decide on the message you want to be known for.

• Place testimonials on your website.

• Have a drawing for a product you are selling. It makes the people in the audience want to have it.

• Decide on fast acting bonuses that you will add to your sales offer.

• Create a risk-free guarantee that takes away the fear of purchase.

CHAPTER 11
IT'S A WRAP

My son Stefan appeared on an episode of the popular television show *Sex & the City*. He was a background extra in a club scene with Sarah Jessica Parker. Now the term background extra implies that you are not a star in the scene. However, extras are needed because they bring the scene to life by giving it character, color and dimension. My son loved the opportunity of being on the show and brought with him his humor and personality. This did not go unnoticed by Sarah Jessica Parker. She told my son that he must not leave the set before she wrote him a note saying he was one of the best extras she ever worked with.

Stefan knows the art of connecting with those around him is the secret to being memorable.

Strong Close

The close of a speech is just as important as the opening. If you want to be memorable with your audience, you must have a strong close. The open and close are what the audience tends to remember.

Give a statement that indicates your speech is drawing to a close so that people fully focus on you. Don't give the typical, "In closing." You want your close to be as creative as your speech. Earlier I mentioned that you should memorize your opening comments. I feel that it is equally important to memorize your close and not leave the wording to chance.

It is strong to close with a story that ties everything together, drives your message home, and creates the desire to work with you. Your story should summarize your key points. You want people to remember the purpose of your talk.

Your speech should create change in your audience so that you are remembered long after everyone goes home. Give your audience an assignment that will reinforce your key points and bring your message to life. I encourage people to move out of their comfort zone and decide to join my movement to become the new face of celebrity by speaking on topics they want to be known for.

A Star Is Born

Do you want to be a Bit Player, Supporting Player or Star in your area of expertise? Only you can make that decision.

If you want to outshine your competition, stay top-of-mind and be known for what you do, speaking can be the vehicle to make that happen. Speaking can skyrocket your career success.

Make the decision to be known. Give yourself permission to follow your dream and shine the spotlight on what you do. Practice your speeches and become great at delivering your performance. It is critical to your success. Think of your talk as a gift to others.

My definition of a STAR is a Speaker that is Topical, Articulate and Recognized!

S = Speaker – You are out there in the limelight, speaking on stages and spreading your message.

T = Topical – Your message is one that your audience wants to hear.

A = Articulate – You use your voice to deliver a sizzling, red hot presentation.

R = Recognized – You are top of mind and the recognized expert in your field.

Encore

Don't limit yourself to 15 minutes of fame. Look for the next opportunity to see your name in lights. How can you maximize the publicity for the event where you just spoke? Many times you will get asked by people in the audience to speak at one of their upcoming events.

If you think your last speech was more fizzle than sizzle, take heart. Not every speech is a blockbuster hit. Perhaps the audience was composed of people you weren't told about, maybe you had an off day, or maybe you gave the speech so many times you forgot to keep it new and exciting for your audience. Whatever the reason, analyze your performance and then get back in the game. Stars know that some movies are a hit while others are a flop. They also know that there is always the next opportunity.

If you want to increase your encore engagements, strive to connect with your audience through the delivery of relevant content that brings them to the edge of their seats. Find interesting ways to involve audience participation. Deliver your speech as if you are giving it for the first time. Keep it fresh and exciting. If you follow these steps, you are well on your way to delivering sizzling, red hot presentations!

The sound of applause fills the room. Shouts of "Bravo!" fills the air as you receive a standing ovation. Take a bow. You are now a little bit famous.

For now, until the next time, the curtain comes down.

KEY POINTS TO REMEMBER

• Connecting with your audience is the secret to being memorable.

• You speech must have a strong close.

• You want your close to be as creative as your speech.

• Your speech should create change in your audience so that you are remembered after everyone goes home.

• Speaking can skyrocket your career success.

• Make the decision to be known.

• A STAR is a Speaker that is Topical, Articulate and Recognized!

• Many times you will get asked by people in the audience to speak at one of their upcoming events.

• To increase encore engagements, connect with your audience by delivering relevant content that brings them to the edge of their seats.

ACTION ITEMS

• Memorize your close and do not leave the wording to chance.

• Think of a way to close with a story that ties the points of your speech together, drives your message home, and creates the desire to work with you.

• Give your audience an assignment that will reinforce your key points and bring your message to life.

• Practice your speeches and become great at delivering your performance.

ABOUT THE AUTHOR

Judy Cohen, a former corporate marketing director, is a presentation expert, speaker, coach, certified seminar leader, and author. She has experience on television, radio and the stage.

Judy owns and runs Red Hot Presentations. She gives her clients the tools to become engaging speakers. Judy has committed her life to helping people learn to speak up and become known as experts in their niche by teaching them the art of crafting and delivering red hot presentations.

Speaking

Judy is available for media appearances and

speaking engagements by arrangement. The topic that she is best known for is "How to Become Famous in Your Niche As A Speaker." We all know there is a lot of buzz and attention on Hollywood celebrities, but Judy believes there's no need to be a star watcher when you can have your own sizzling lifestyle and become a little bit famous in your niche. She will teach your group how to position themselves for fame and fortune through the art of speaking.

Red Hot Presentations Programs

Judy's group coaching program, is designed to help position YOU as a star in your niche through the art of presenting.

It's an in-depth program where you will learn how to deliver a speech authentically so that you reach more people with your message, have raving fans, and become sought after in your area of expertise. This program is for you if you want to use speaking to grow your business.

If you would like to work on writing your script, and all aspects of giving a speech, private coaching is available.

If you are ready to go from unknown to center

stage and be known as an expert in your field, Judy can help you change the way you position yourself and your business. She will give you the tools to become the speaker everyone remembers.

A Gift For You

Judy has a free downloadable gift for everyone who visits her Red Hot Presentations website. Go to www.RedHotPresentations.com.

While on the website you can learn more about her events and programs.